Kylie Jean

Pirate Craft Queen

by Mary Meinking and Marci Peschke

illustrated by Tuesday Mourning

PICTURE WINDOW BOOKS
a capstone imprint

Editor: Shelly Lyons
Designer: Tracy Davies McCabe
Craft Project Creator: Marcy Morin
Photo Stylist: Sarah Schuette
Art Director: Nathan Gassman
Production Specialist: Laura Manthe

All photos by Capstone Studio/Karon Dubke
Design elements: Shutterstock

Picture Window Books are published by Capstone,
1710 Roe Crest Drive,
North Mankato, Minnesota 56003
www.capstonepub.com

Library of Congress Cataloging-in-Publication Data
Meinking, Mary and Marci Peschke.
Kylie Jean pirate craft queen /
by Mary Meinking and Marci Peschke.
pages cm — (Nonfiction picture books. Kylie Jean
craft queen.)
Audience: Age 7-9.
Audience: Grades K to 3.
Summary: "Introduces crafts related to the book Kylie
Jean pirate queen, by Marci Peschke"— Provided
by publisher.
Includes bibliographical references and index.
ISBN 978-1-4795-2192-0 (library binding)
1. Handicraft—Juvenile literature. 2. Pirates—
Folklore—Juvenile literature. I. Peschke, M. (Marci).
Pirate queen. II. Title. III. Title: Pirate craft queen.
TT160.M423 2014
745.5—dc23   2013032216

Photo Credits
All photos by Capstone Studio/Karon Dubke
Design elements: Shutterstock

Printed in the United States of America in Brainerd, Minnesota.
092013   007770BANGS14

Table of Contents

Ahoy!

All hands on deck for crafts! It's me, Kylie Jean, the Pirate Queen. I just know my mates will love this book full of fun ideas. When you get done with these projects you'll have everything a pirate needs. One of my favorite crafts is the pink glitter eye patch. When I wear it, I want to shout, "Shiver me timbers!"

You can make a fishbowl, something for your dog, or a real true treasure chest for your jewelry. Blimey! Everything is so easy—you'll want to make them all!

TOOLS NEEDED

- adhesive-backed magnet strips
- chalk
- duct tape or masking tape
- fabric glue
- fabric scissors
- foam glue
- foam paintbrush
- glitter glue
- hole punch
- hot glue gun
- markers
- metal binder ring
- paintbrush
- pen
- pencil
- puffy paint
- ruler
- stapler
- tempera paint
- washable markers
- white glue

TIPS

- Before starting a project, read all of the steps and gather all of the supplies needed.
- Work on newspaper or paper towels.
- Ask an adult to help you use a hot glue gun and sharp tools.
- Give glue and paint plenty of time to dry before handling a project.

Hidden Treasure Bag

You can add beads, rhinestones, or sequins to this treasure bag to make it really special. Then keep all your pirate gold or booty (I mean your allowance) in it!

You will need:

- 9x12-inch (23x30-centimeter) pink felt sheet
- pen
- ruler
- large plate or bowl
- fabric scissors
- hole punch
- white puffy paint or fabric paint
- thin ribbon or cording
- pony bead

Optional:
- rhinestones

---

1. Draw a 9-inch (23-cm) circle on the felt by tracing around a large plate or bowl. Cut out.

2. With the hole punch, punch holes around the edge of the circle, ¾ inch (1.9 cm) in from the edge and 1 inch (2.5 cm) apart. Cut away any hole punches that don't fall out on their own.

3. With the white paint, draw a 1 ½-inch-(3.8-cm-) tall skull and crossbones. Start near the holes, and make the chin closest to the center. Let dry.

4. Fold the tip of the ribbon in half. With the skull and crossbones facing away from you, thread the ribbon downward through a hole. Thread it upward through the next hole. Continue stringing the ribbon through the holes, ending with both ends going downward through the same hole.

5. Pull the ribbon ends to make them the same length. Push both ends through a pony bead, and push the bead up next to the felt.

Optional: Glue rhinestones onto the bag and ribbon. Let dry.

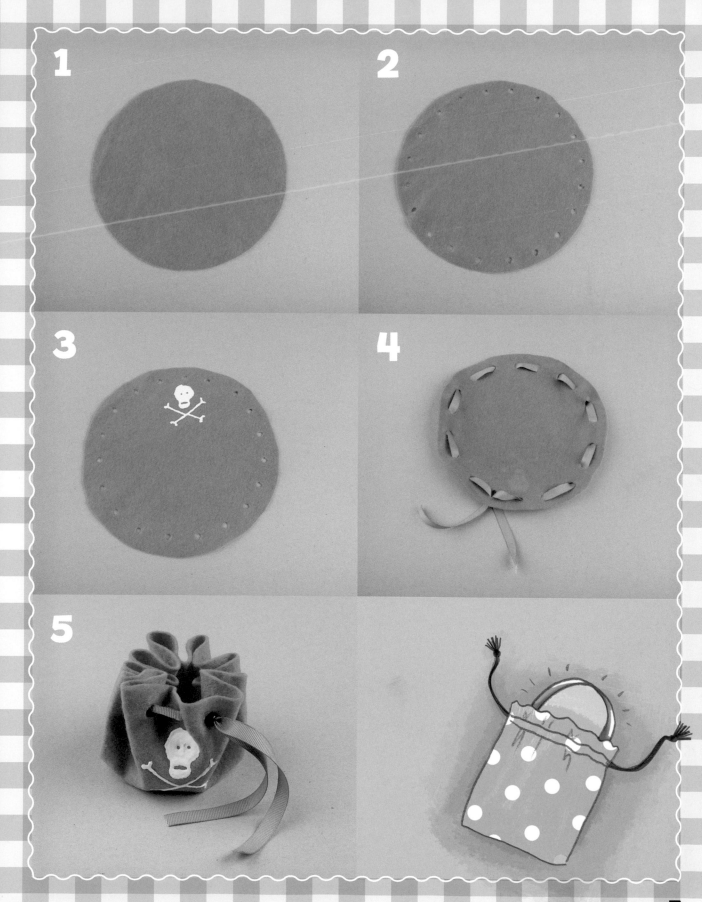

Bart Black's Eye Patch

This is one of my favorite crafts! I love pink, and you'll finish making this patch quick as a wink. When I tried it on, I shouted, "Shiver me timbers!"

You will need:

- 3x3-inch (7.6x7.6-cm) piece of black felt
- chalk
- ruler
- fabric scissors
- hot glue
- thin black elastic headband
- pink puffy paint
- silver glitter glue

Optional:
- 2 small wiggly eyes
- thin pink ribbon

1. On the felt, draw a 2 ½-inch (6.4-cm) by 1 ¾-inch (4.4-cm) "D" with chalk. Stack two pieces of felt on top of each other. Cut out both pieces at the same time.

2. Separate the pieces. Draw a line of glue ⅜ inch (1 cm) from the top straight edge of one piece. Press the headband into the glue. Draw a line of glue around the edge of the other piece, and sandwich that piece over the headband, lining up the edges of the two felt pieces. Let dry.

3. With the pink puffy paint, draw a skull and crossbones on the outside felt piece.

4. Add glitter around the edge of the felt. Let dry.

Optional: Press wiggly eyes into the wet skull paint. Let dry. Glue on a thin pink ribbon bow.

Hint:
If the headband is too big to hold the patch over the eye, tie a knot at the back of the band to shorten.

1

2

3

4

Optional

Jolly Roger Flag

Pirates call this flag a Jolly Roger, but I call it a Jolly Jean! Make yours pink like mine. You don't even have to sew to make it.

You will need:

- 9x12-inch (23x31-cm) white felt sheet
- pencil
- fabric scissors
- fabric glue
- 9x12-inch (23x31-cm) pink felt sheet
- small square black felt
- 6 inches (15 cm) thin black ribbon
- black marker
- stick or wooden dowel

Optional:
- glitter glue
- rhinestones
- gemstone

1. Draw a skull and crossbones on white felt. Cut out.

2. Glue the skull and crossbones to the pink felt sheet.

3. Cut a small "D" out of the black felt for an eye patch. Glue it to the skull. Let dry.

4. Cut ribbon to the width of the skull. Glue it above the eye patch. Use the black marker to draw an eye, nose, and mouth on the skull.

5. Wrap the left edge of the flag around the stick. Glue in place. Let dry.

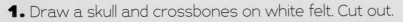

Optional: Use glitter glue to add a sparkly border to the flag. Glue rhinestones to the flag. Add a gemstone for an eye.

You can download a free template for this craft at capstonekids.com.

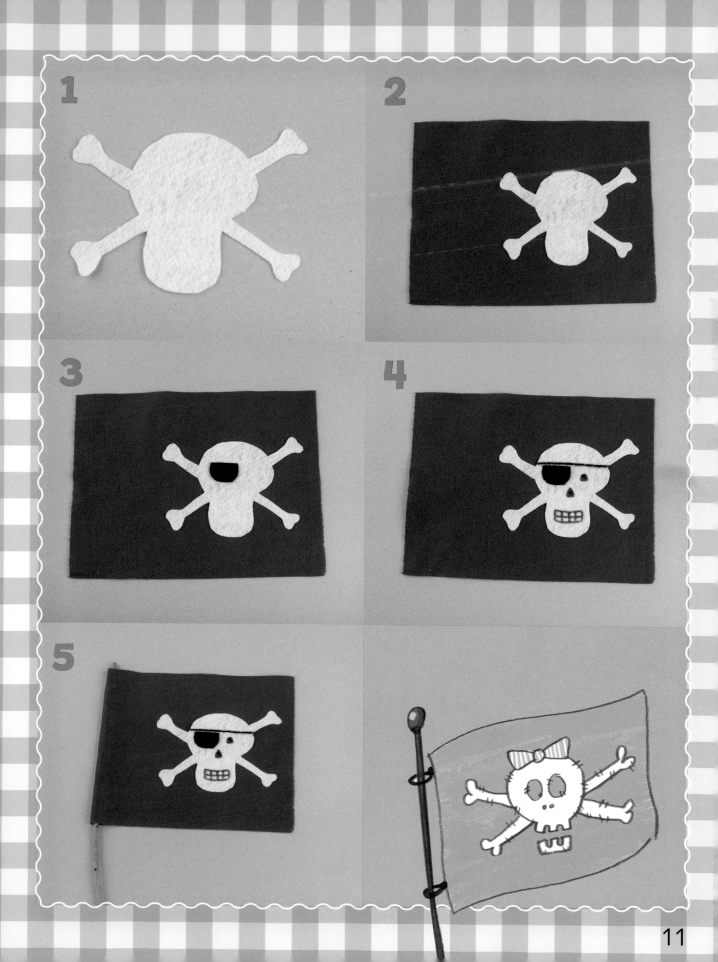

Tied-Up Sash

You'll have this project tied up in no time! This sash is fantastic. Make it with beads, and wear it on swashbuckling days!

You will need:

- ¼ yard (23 cm) cotton fabric, 45 inches (114 cm) wide or wider
- chalk
- ruler
- fabric scissors
- pony beads
- hot glue gun
- 2, 3-foot (91-cm) strips of glitter ribbon
- 3-foot (.9-m) strip of stringed beading

Optional:
- liquid seam sealant

1. Fold fabric in half lengthwise, with finished edges together. Lay on a flat surface. With chalk, make tick marks 5 inches (13 cm) in from the cut edge.

2. Use the ruler to connect the marks. Cut on the line through both layers of fabric. This piece will be your sash.

3. Mark a line 3 inches (7.6 cm) in from each short end.

4. Cut from the end to the line, about every ¼ inch (.64 cm). Repeat on the other end.

5. String a bead on every other fringe string. Fold the tip of each fringe piece in half to make it easier to push through the bead hole. Tie a knot under each bead. Repeat on the opposite end.

6. Hot glue the two strips of glitter ribbon about 1 inch (2.5 cm) apart down the length of the sash. Hot glue the stringed beading down the middle of the sash.

Optional: Coat the long sides of the sash with liquid seam sealant to prevent the edges from unraveling. Let dry.

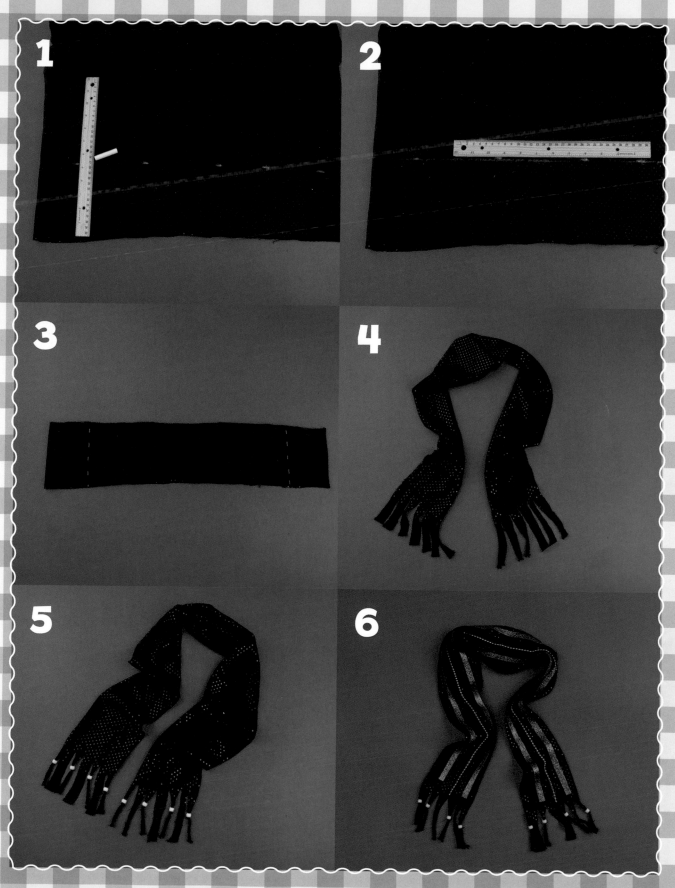

Treasure Chest Jewelry Box

Pirates need a special spot to hide their jewels. I made this treasure box, and so can you! Just be sure to keep it away from my dog, Ugly Brother!

You will need:

- hinged-lid shoebox
- ruler
- 22x28-inch (56x71-cm) sheet pink poster board
- pencil
- scissors
- hot glue
- silver duct tape
- silver foam sheet
- foam glue

Optional:
- rhinestones
- black marker

1. Measure the width of the front of the shoebox. On the poster board, mark a line the same width down the entire shorter side. Cut on that line.

2. Starting at the inside of the lid in front, wrap the poster board around to the front bottom edge of the box. Leave a rounded arch on the top of the lid. Mark this length on the poster board, and cut. Wrap the poster board around again, and hot glue it to the box.

3. Measure and cut a rectangle from the remaining poster board to cover the front part of the box. Glue it to the box.

4. Measure and cut two rectangles the size of the small ends of the box. Glue on.

5. Trace around the arch and box lid onto the poster board. Draw a small tab on the top and both sides of the arched piece. Draw a straight line to connect both ends of the drawn arch. Cut out. Use this piece to trace and cut out a second arched piece and tabs.

6. Fold down the three tabs on each piece. Glue the bottom of the piece to the lid, and glue each tab to the arch.

7. Cut a piece of duct tape the length of the whole arched lid. Cut the tape in half lengthwise. Starting at the lid opening, stick half the width of tape to the treasure chest, with the other half hanging over. Cut the tape every 1 inch (2.5 cm) in the arched part. Press tape down. Repeat on the other side. Cover the lower corner edges in the front and back of the chest with the half-width tape as well.

8. Cut 1 ¼-inch- (3.2-cm-) wide strips of the silver foam. Cut two pieces to the length of the arched lid, from the front to the hinge in the back. Glue the strips over the arched lid with foam glue. Glue additional pieces to the front (going under the lid) and back of the base. Let dry.

Optional: Hot glue rhinestones to the top arched silver straps. Cut out a rounded silver foam rectangle. Draw on a key hole. Glue to the front, center lid of your treasure chest.

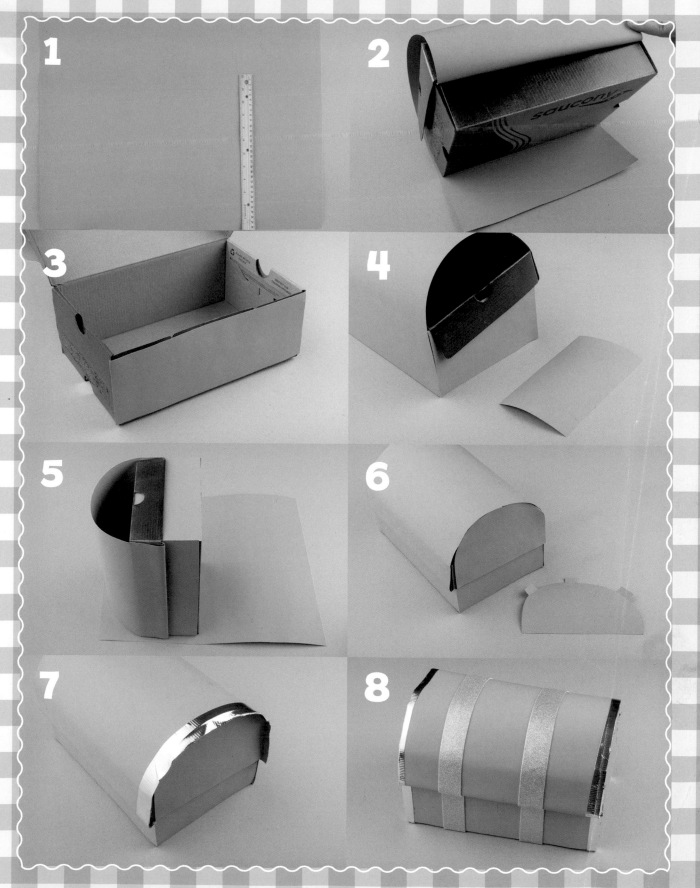

Pirate Mask

I love to pretend, and I bet y'all do too! Make these masks with your crew. Then put on a pirate play. My pirate mask has a pink bandana!

You will need:

- paper plate
- flesh color tempera paint
- paintbrush
- 14x4 ½-inch (36x11-cm) pink cotton fabric
- ruler
- pencil
- fabric scissors
- water bottle cap
- paper scissors
- glue
- black felt
- thin black ribbon
- markers
- paper punch
- metal binder ring
- wooden paint stir stick
- duct tape

1. Paint two-thirds of the plate on the back, domed side. Let dry.

2. Glue the fabric to the remaining part of the plate. Let dry. Flip the plate and fabric over. Cut the fabric around the plate edge, leaving a 2-inch (5-cm) tall by 4-inch (10-cm) long tail on one side. Cut the tail in half the long way. Tie a knot in it.

3. Make eye holes by tracing around the water bottle cap to make two circles on the face. Leave about 1 ¼ inches (3.2 cm) between them. Cut out.

4. Draw a 2 ½-inch (6.4-cm) by 1 ¾-inch (4.4-cm) "D" on the black felt. Cut out

and glue onto the pirate mask over one cutout circle. Let dry.

5. Measure the ribbon the length of the plate. Cut and glue the ribbon to line the pink fabric and the eye patch below.

6. With markers, draw a nose and mouth.

7. Punch a hole, ¼ inch (.64 cm) from the edge of the face on the opposite side of the bandana tie. Open the binder ring and slide through the hole. Snap it closed.

8. Tape the top third of the stir stick to the bottom back of the mask.

Hint:
To start cutting out the eye circles, make a small fold at the center of the circle.

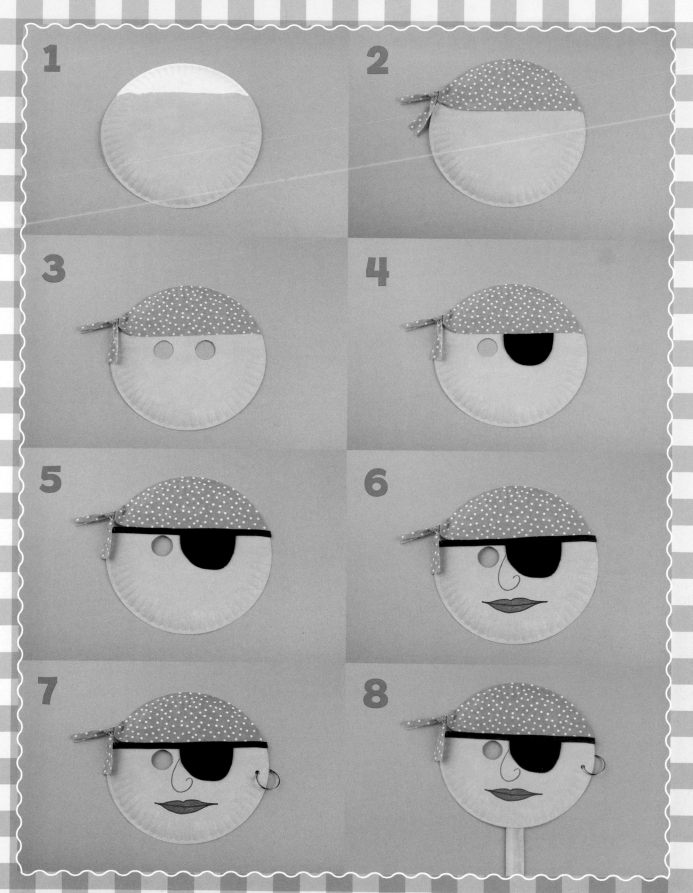

17

Pirate's Hat

I have a pirate hat decorated with a pink feather and a skull and crossbones. When I wear it, I shout, "A crafting captain I will be. It's a crafter's life for me!"

You will need:

- 2, 12x18-inch (31x46-cm) sheets black construction paper
- scissors
- large pink feather
- stapler
- white construction paper
- pencil
- black marker
- hot glue
- wiggly eye
- thin pink ribbon
- string of rhinestones

1. Stack the black sheets of paper on top of one another. Fold the sheets in half width-wise. Draw half of a pirate hat shape, and cut out. Unfold both hats.

2. Restack the hats on top of one another. Sandwich the feather between them. Staple the two hat shapes together around the edge, leaving the bottom open. Staple the feather in place.

3. Draw a skull and crossbones on the white paper. Draw a nose and teeth onto the skull. Cut out and glue to the front of the hat. Use black marker to draw an eye patch.

4. Glue a wiggly eye onto the skull. Let dry.

5. Tie a loose knot in the center of the ribbon. Hot glue the ribbon to the top of the skull.

6. Measure a string of rhinestones the length of the outer edge of the hat. Cut the string to the length, and hot glue to the edge of the hat.

Hint:
If the hat is too big to stay on your head, add one staple on each side of hat, near the straight, bottom edge.

You can download a free template for this craft at capstonekids.com.

Hidden Treasure Map

This treasure map project doubles as a fun place mat! It is more fun than singing sea shanties, so get creative! I even drew a compass rose.

You will need:

- 12 ½x6-inch (32x15-cm) (folded flat) brown paper bag
- washable markers
- paintbrush
- water
- pencil

Optional:
- contact paper

1. Tear along the glued seam on the back of the bag, to the bottom of the bag.

2. Open the bag, and tear along the bottom edge all the way around the bag. Discard the bottom piece of the bag. Tear the bag in half to create two 9 ½-inch (24-cm) by 12-inch (30-cm) rectangles. Set one aside.

3. Wrinkle up the paper bag rectangle. Flatten out. With the brown marker, draw a rough wide border all around the paper, overlapping the edge. Wet the paintbrush, and blend the brown marker into the paper. Let dry.

4. Use the pencil to draw out your treasure map. Include: water, an island, a pirate ship, trees, a treasure chest, and a compass rose. Draw a border around the map, near the brown edge. Use markers to color in your map.

Optional: Cover with contact paper to use as a place mat.

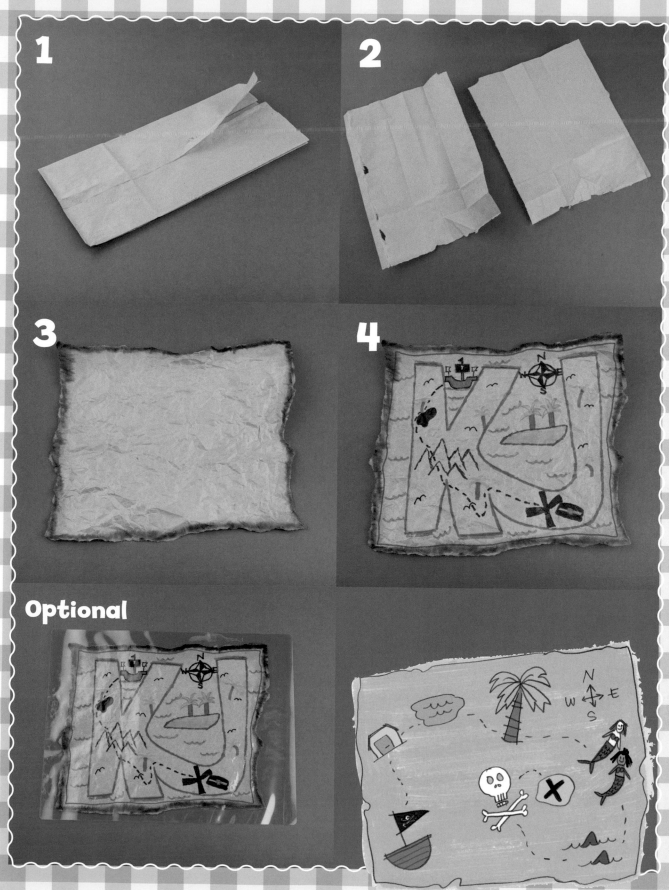

1

2

3

4

Optional

21

Dog Treat Holder

To complete my pirate look, my dog, Ugly Brother, dresses as a parrot. Let's give him parrot wings for this dog treat holder. Y'all, there is no better place for doggie treats!

You will need:

- 2, 9-inch (23-cm) paper plates
- pencil
- scissors
- black and pink markers
- stapler
- paper

- 2 pieces each of 3 colors of construction paper
- rhinestones
- 2 wiggly eyes
- white glue

Optional:
- thin ribbon

---

1. With pencil, draw the bulldog's face on the back, domed side of one of the paper plates. Leave the top of its head and ears flat. Cut off the top edge along the dog's head. With markers, draw the face.

2. Line up the edges of the other paper plate with the cut out piece, creating a pocket. Staple the plates together in three places. Trace the top cutout part of the dog's head to the plain plate. Cut off.

3. Place two pieces of the same color of construction paper on top of each other. Trace a three-part wing onto the top piece, and cut out both pieces. Repeat with the two other colors.

4. Layer and staple the wing pieces.

5. Slide the stapled top part of each wing between the paper plates. Staple in place. Glue rhinestones to the dog's collar. Let dry.

6. Glue the wiggly eyes to the dog's face.

Optional: Glue ribbon ends to the top of the back plate for hanging. Let dry.

You can download a free template for this craft at capstonekids.com.

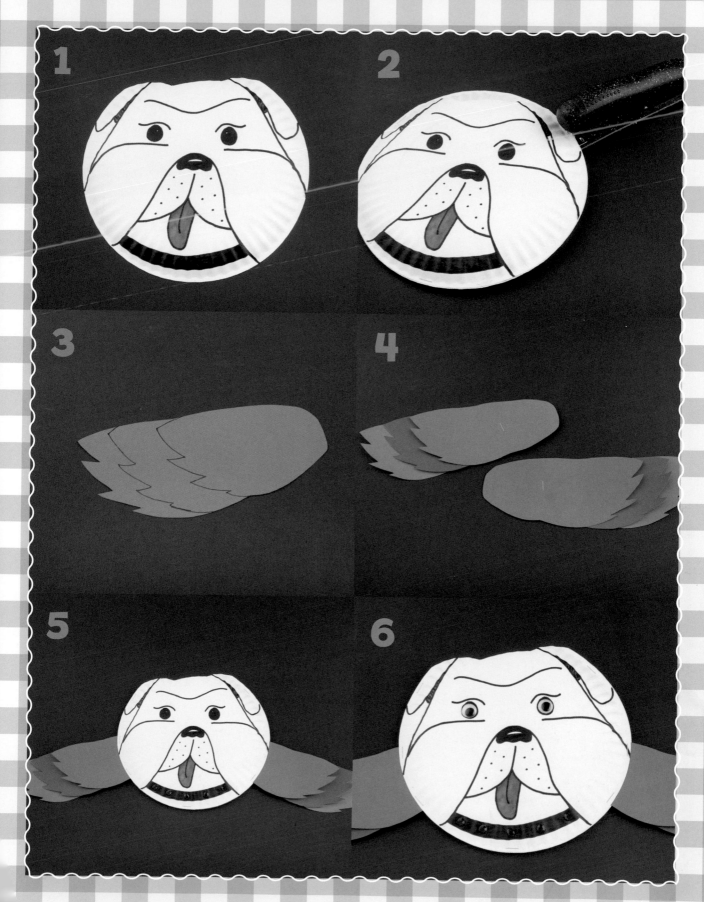

23

Trick or Treat Loot Bag

Trick or treat, this bag is neat! Take it when you go door-to-door looking for candy and goodies on Halloween. Make one for a friend too!

You will need:

- paper
- pencil
- scissors
- black fabric
- white felt
- fabric scissors
- pink cloth grocery or tote bag
- white glue or fabric glue
- black marker
- white puffy paint
- large wiggly eye

Optional:
- rhinestones
- thin ribbon or lace

1. Fold the paper in half. Draw half of a skull, eye patch, and pirate hat. Cut out each piece and unfold. Trace the hat and patch onto fabric, and the skull onto felt. Cut out.

2. Arrange the pieces on the cloth bag, and glue in place. Let dry.

3. Use marker to draw the eye patch cord at the top of the patch to the sides of the skull.

4. Use puffy paint to draw the crossbones and the top hat trim. Let dry.

5. Glue on the wiggly eye. Let dry.

Optional: Draw a nose and mouth on the skull with marker. Glue rhinestones to the bag. Let dry. Add ribbon or lace trim to the edges. Tie ribbons on the handles.

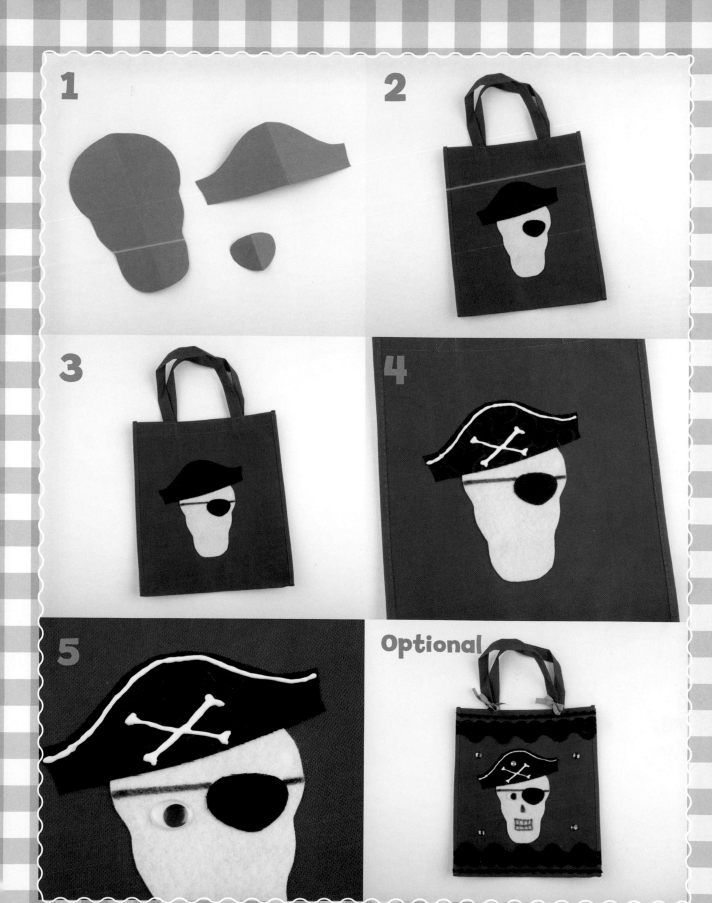

Pumpkin Magnetic Frame

This frame is so cute! Make one for each of your family members, and have a pumpkin patch! I made one for my dog, Ugly Brother. He tried to eat it!

You will need:

- paper
- pencil
- ruler
- scissors
- 2 each, white and black foam sheets
- black marker
- thin ribbon
- foam glue
- white puffy paint
- wiggly eye
- 2 short strips of adhesive-backed magnets

optional:
- rhinestones

1. Draw a pumpkin shape on paper, about 4 ½ inches (11 cm) by 7 inches (18 cm). Toward the top, add a bandana knot off to one side of the pumpkin. Cut out. Trace onto two pieces of white foam. Draw a large pumpkin smile toward the bottom on one piece. Outline this piece with black marker. Cut out both pieces.

2. Draw a pirate's hat, approximately 5 ½ inches (14 cm) by 2 inches (5 cm) on paper. Also draw a "D"-shaped eye patch, approximately 1 ¼ inch (3.2 cm) by 1 inch (2.5 cm). Cut out. Trace on black foam, and cut out.

3. Measure the ribbon to the width of the pumpkin. Cut and glue to the pumpkin, so it will sit right below the edge of the hat.

4. Glue the two pieces of white foam together, close to the edge on three sides, but leave the top unglued. Let dry.

5. Using white puffy paint, draw a skull and crossbones on the hat. Add an outline around the top of the hat. Let dry.

6. Glue eye patch and wiggly eye on pumpkin. Let dry.

7. With black marker, draw the eye patch string from both sides of the patch to the edges of the pumpkin.

8. Glue the hat onto the pumpkin. Let dry.

9. Stick the magnets to the back of the pumpkin.

Optional: Add rhinestones to the eye patch. Slide a picture into the frame, and stick to your refrigerator.

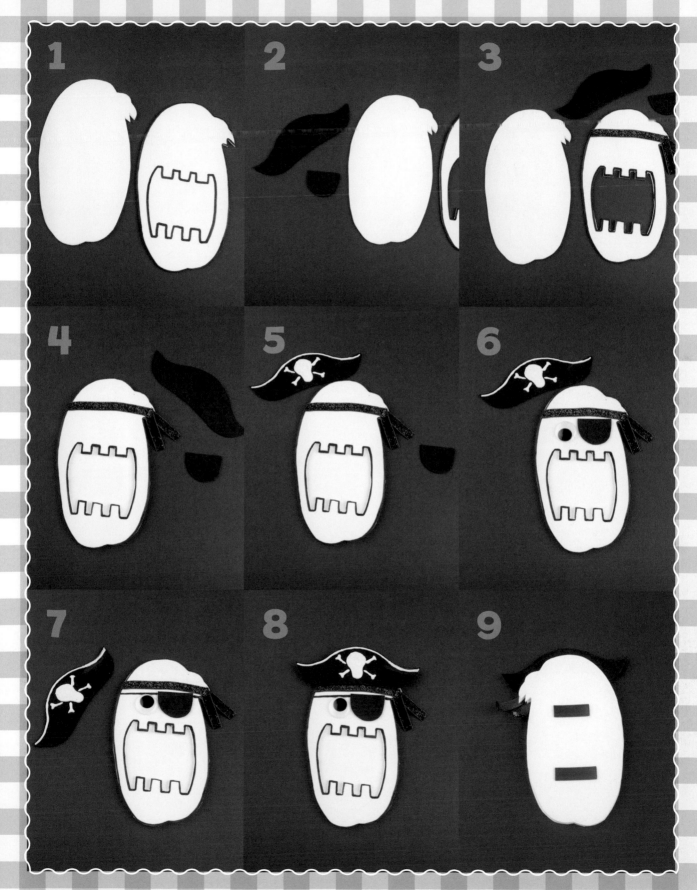

Bart Black's Big Old, Creepy House

What's more fun than a dollhouse? Bart Black's old, creepy house! You can make it all by yourself, but it's pretty creepy! Maybe you should invite some friends to make one too!

You will need:

- stapler
- clean milk carton (pint to half-gallon)
- construction paper (pink, black, brown, purple)
- pencil
- scissors
- white glue
- markers
- cotton ball

1. Staple the top of the carton closed. Lay the carton on its side with the pointed top facing down on the pink paper. Trace around it. Connect the tip to where the sides start (creating a triangle top). Make each side piece slightly wider than the carton, so no carton will show through when pieced together. Cut out two of these pieces.

2. Lay the carton on a squared-off side. Trace around it, but make it 1 inch (2.5 cm) taller. Cut out two of these pieces.

3. Glue the squared off pieces to their proper sides. Make sure the taller pieces are glued onto the slanted parts of the carton. Repeat with the pointed top pieces. Let dry.

4. Cut a black rectangle for the roof that's folded in the middle. Let it hang over the edges on all four sides. Glue on the roof, and let dry.

5. Draw windows on yellow paper with brown or black markers. Add thinner window panes and boards over some windows. Cut out, and glue on. Let dry.

6. Make a door from the brown paper. Cut out, and glue on. Cut out shutters for the windows, and glue on. Let dry.

7. Draw lines on the house to make siding. Pull out a few fibers from the cotton ball. Glue onto the house. Let dry.

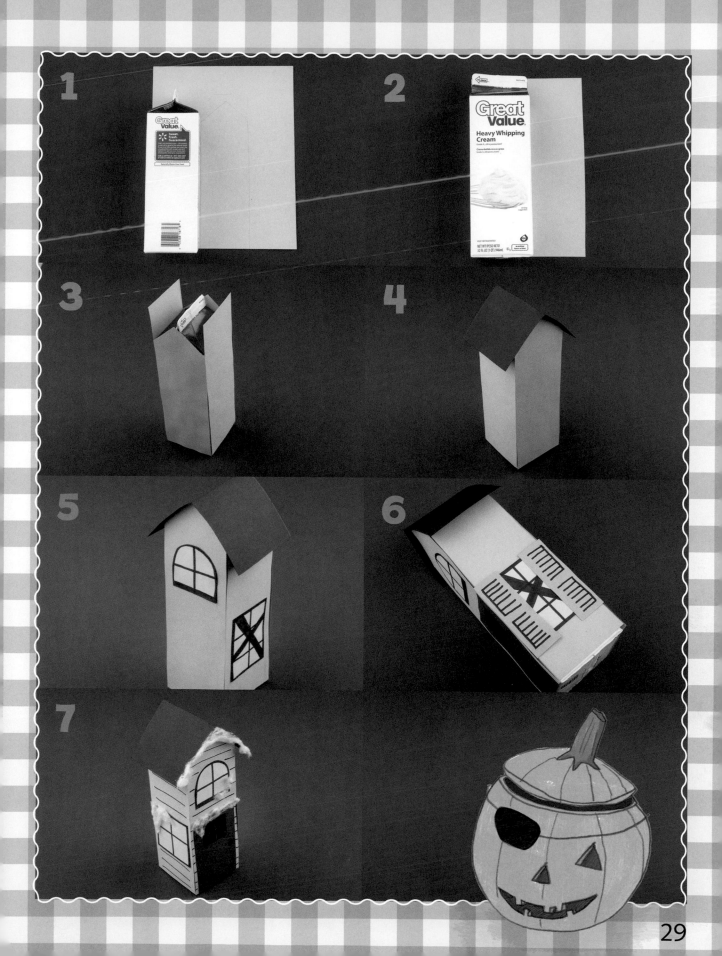

Light-Up Fishbowl

What a perfect place for a paper pet fish! When you are finished adding your details, you can pretend that the glitter is fish food. Sprinkle in lots of sparkle!

You will need:

- colored tissue papers
- pencil
- ruler
- scissors
- white glue and water (or decoupage liquid)
- glass fishbowl
- small foam paintbrush
- disposable cup
- glitter
- rocks or marbles

Optional:
- battery-operated tea light candle

1. On the orange tissue paper, draw a goldfish, approximately 3 ½ inches (8.9 cm) by 2 inches (5 cm). Cut out. On the black tissue paper, draw a sunken pirate ship, approximately 3 ½ inches (8.9 cm) by 1 ½ inches (3.8 cm). Cut out. Cut out several green, grass-like seaweed tissue paper pieces. Glue the goldfish across from the sunken ship, on the inside of the fishbowl. Glue the seaweed at the bottom.

2. Tear several 1-inch (2.5-cm) by 2-inch (5-cm) strips of blue tissue paper.

3. In the cup, mix together 3 parts glue with 1 part warm water. Use the brush to mix. Paint a small area on the inside of the bowl with the glue, and press the torn blue tissue horizontally into the glue. Repeat until the entire inside is covered with tissue. Overlapping tissue is good. Coat the inside with glue, pressing down the tissue paper. Sprinkle glitter into the bowl for sparkle. Let dry.

4. Fill the bottom with rocks or marbles.

Optional: Place a battery-operated tea light on top of the rocks.

You can download a free template for this craft at capstonekids.com.

Read More

Llimós Plomer, Anna. *Pirate Ship Adventure Crafts.* Fun Adventure Crafts. Berkeley Heights, N.J.: Enslow Elementary, 2011.

Peschke, Marci. *Pirate Queen.* Kylie Jean. North Mankato, Minn.: Picture Window Books, 2013.

Shirley, Rebekah Joy. *I Want to Be a Pirate.* Let's Play Dress Up. New York: Windmill Books, 2012.

Internet Sites

FactHound offers a safe, fun way to find Internet sites related to this book. All of the sites on FactHound have been researched by our staff.

Here's all you do:

Visit *www.facthound.com*

Type in this code: 9781479521920

Super-cool stuff!

Check out projects, games and lots more at
www.capstonekids.com

Look for all the books in the series:

Party Craft Queen   Rodeo Craft Queen

Pirate Craft Queen   Summer Camp Craft Queen